ALL AROUND THE WORLD
SCOTLAND

by Kristine Spanier

pogo

Ideas for Parents and Teachers

Pogo Books let children practice reading informational text while introducing them to nonfiction features such as headings, labels, sidebars, maps, and diagrams, as well as a table of contents, glossary, and index.

Carefully leveled text with a strong photo match offers early fluent readers the support they need to succeed.

Before Reading

- "Walk" through the book and point out the various nonfiction features. Ask the student what purpose each feature serves.
- Look at the glossary together. Read and discuss the words.

Read the Book

- Have the child read the book independently.
- Invite him or her to list questions that arise from reading.

After Reading

- Discuss the child's questions. Talk about how he or she might find answers to those questions.
- Prompt the child to think more. Ask: The Highland Games attract many visitors to Scotland each year. What special events do you attend where you live?

Pogo Books are published by Jump!
5357 Penn Avenue South
Minneapolis, MN 55419
www.jumplibrary.com

Library of Congress Cataloging-in-Publication Data

Names: Spanier, Kristine, author.
Title: Scotland / by Kristine Spanier.
Description: Minneapolis, MN : Jump!, Inc., 2020.
Series: All Around the World | "Pogo Books."
Includes bibliographical references and index.
Identifiers: LCCN 2018046615 (print)
LCCN 2018047619 (ebook)
ISBN 9781641286558 (e-book)
ISBN 9781641286527 (hardcover : alk. paper)
ISBN 9781641286541 (pbk.)
Subjects: LCSH: Scotland—Juvenile literature.
Classification: LCC DA762 (ebook)
LCC DA762 .S57 2020 (print) | DDC 941.1—dc23
LC record available at https://lccn.loc.gov/2018046615

Editor: Susanne Bushman
Designer: Molly Ballanger

Photo Credits: simonbradfield/iStock, cover; Route66/Shutterstock, 1; Pixfiction/Shutterstock, 3; Eldredd Chester/Shutterstock, 4; argalis/iStock, 5; majeczka/Shutterstock, 6-7 (background); Antonio Coppola/Shutterstock, 6-7 (foreground); Shaiith/Shutterstock, 8t; Doptis/Shutterstock, 8b; Neil Burton/Shutterstock, 8-9t; Enrique Aguirre/Shutterstock, 8-9b; Colin McPherson/Getty, 10; Scottish Viewpoint/Alamy, 11; George KUZ/Shutterstock, 12-13; WPA Pool/Getty, 14-15; Joerg Beuge/Shutterstock, 16 (soup); Natalia Mylova/Shutterstock, 16 (bowl); mahirart/Shutterstock, 16 (leeks); stockcreations/Shutterstock, 17; VisitBritain/Andrew Pickett/Getty, 18-19; Philip Brown/Getty, 20-21; incamerastock/Alamy, 23.

Printed in the United States of America at Corporate Graphics in North Mankato, Minnesota.

TABLE OF CONTENTS

CHAPTER 1
Welcome to Scotland! 4

CHAPTER 2
Life in Scotland 10

CHAPTER 3
Food and Fun 16

QUICK FACTS & TOOLS
At a Glance 22
Glossary 23
Index 24
To Learn More 24

CHAPTER 1

WELCOME TO SCOTLAND!

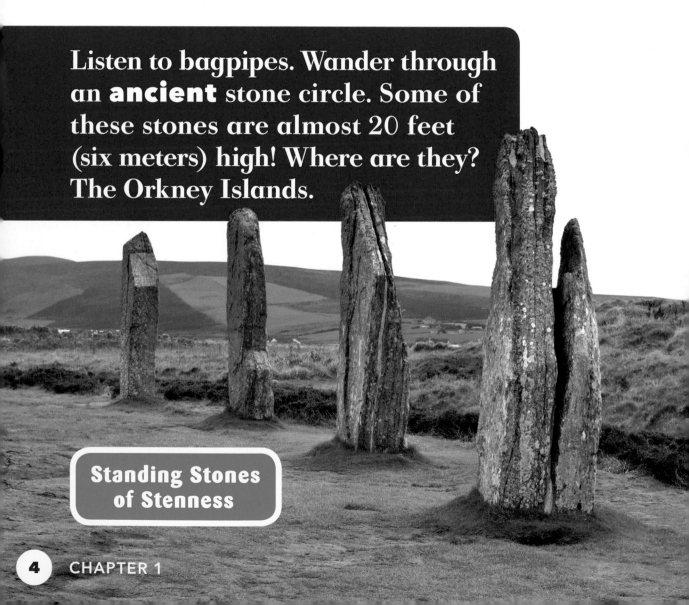

Listen to bagpipes. Wander through an **ancient** stone circle. Some of these stones are almost 20 feet (six meters) high! Where are they? The Orkney Islands.

Standing Stones of Stenness

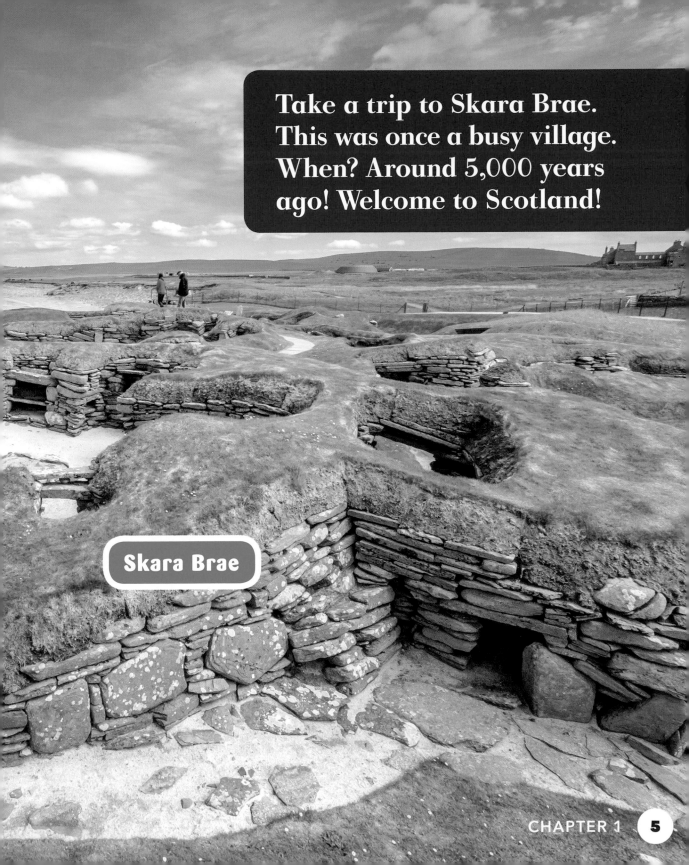

Take a trip to Skara Brae. This was once a busy village. When? Around 5,000 years ago! Welcome to Scotland!

Skara Brae

Scotland is part of the United Kingdom. It is north of England. Kings and queens once lived in castles here. Edinburgh Castle is one. It stands on a hill called Castle Rock.

Edinburgh
Castle

highland cow

Atlantic seal

orca whale

gannet

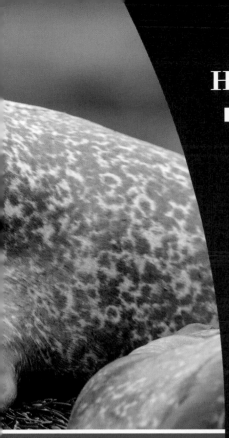

Highland cows are common in **rural** areas. Atlantic seals swim in the waters. Dolphins and porpoises, too. You could see whales! Spot gulls. Gannets. Fulmars. What are these? Seabirds. They fly along the coast.

WHAT DO YOU THINK?

Nature **reserves** here keep **endangered** animals safe. Like what? The pine marten. The golden eagle. The Scottish wildcat. Are there endangered animals near you? How can you help protect them?

CHAPTER 2
LIFE IN SCOTLAND

Children here go to school for at least 12 years. They may leave when they are 16 years old. But most continue school. They prepare for jobs or college.

Many work in **tourism**.
Others build computers.
Or other electronics.
Farming is also important.
What else? Fishing.

Loch Ness

The busiest cities are in the south. This area is called the Central Lowlands. Glasgow is the largest city. It is a **port**.

The Highlands are north. Many lakes are here. They call them lochs. Loch Ness is one of the biggest. Some say a sea monster lives in this lake!

DID YOU KNOW?

Crops grow in the rural areas. Which crops? Oats. Wheat. Potatoes. The hills are good for raising **livestock**.

The head of the government is the United Kingdom's **prime minister**. Scotland has representatives in the U.K. **parliament**. It meets in London. They make laws.

Scotland also has its own parliament. It meets in Edinburgh. This is the **capital**.

The **sovereign** of the United Kingdom has a home here, too. He or she approves the laws and attends special events.

Scottish Parliament

CHAPTER 3

FOOD AND FUN

Would you like to try cock-a-leekie soup? It is full of leeks! These are vegetables similar to onions.

leek

haggis

Haggis is popular. It is made of sheep, oats, and spices. Porridge is a filling breakfast. Or enjoy some scones. Shortbread, too! Yum!

The Highland Games take place every year. People play bagpipes. They dance. They take part in sports, too.

Many wear kilts at these games! You will see many **tartans**. Stripes of different colors cross each other. There are many patterns!

kilt •••••▶

TAKE A LOOK!

The Highland Games have different contests. Here are some of the sports!

caber toss

hammer throw

shot put

tug-of-war

Soccer is a popular sport here. They call it football. People play rugby and cricket, too. Many people also enjoy hiking in the hills. Fun!

Many adventures are waiting in Scotland. Do you want to visit?

WHAT DO YOU THINK?

The Old Course in St. Andrews is the oldest golf course in the world! People have played on it since the 1500s! Have you ever played golf? Would you like to?

cricket

QUICK FACTS & TOOLS

SCOTLAND

Location: western Europe

Size: 30,421 square miles (78,789 square kilometers)

Population: 5,404,700 (July 2018 estimate)

Capital: Edinburgh

Type of Government: parliamentary constitutional monarchy

Language: English

Exports: food, beverages, electronics, petroleum products

Currency: pound sterling

GLOSSARY

ancient: Very old.

capital: A city where government leaders meet.

crops: Plants grown for food.

endangered: In danger of becoming extinct, usually because of human activity.

livestock: Animals that are kept or raised on a farm or ranch.

parliament: A group of people elected to make laws.

port: A town with a harbor where ships can load and unload goods.

prime minister: The leader of a country.

reserves: Protected places where hunting is not allowed and where animals can live and breed safely.

rural: Related to the country and country life.

sovereign: A king or queen.

tartans: Patterns for cloth made of crossing stripes of various widths and colors.

tourism: The business of serving people who are traveling for pleasure.

Scotland's currency

INDEX

animals 9

bagpipes 4, 18

capital 14

Central Lowlands 13

crops 13

Edinburgh 14

Edinburgh Castle 6

England 6

food 16, 17

Glasgow 13

Highland Games 18, 19

Highlands 13

Loch Ness 13

Orkney Islands 4

parliament 14

prime minister 14

reserves 9

school 10

Skara Brae 5

sports 18, 19, 20

St. Andrews 20

tartans 18

tourism 11

United Kingdom 6, 14

TO LEARN MORE

Finding more information is as easy as 1, 2, 3.

❶ Go to www.factsurfer.com

❷ Enter "Scotland" into the search box.

❸ Click the "Surf" button to see a list of websites.

FACT SURFER